A

RUDOLF STEINER (1861–1925) called his spiritual philosophy 'anthroposophy', meaning 'wisdom of the human being'. As a highly developed seer, he based his work on direct knowledge and perception of spiritual dimensions. He initiated a modern and universal 'science of spirit', accessible to anyone willing to exercise clear and unprejudiced thinking.

From his spiritual investigations Steiner provided suggestions for the renewal of many activities, including education (both general and special), agriculture, medicine, economics, architecture, science, philosophy, religion and the arts. Today there are thousands of schools, clinics, farms and other organizations involved in practical work based on his principles. His many published works feature his research into the spiritual nature of the human being, the evolution of the world and humanity, and methods of personal development. Steiner wrote some 30 books and delivered over 6,000 lectures across Europe. In 1924 he founded the General Anthroposophical Society, which today has branches throughout the world.

THE DEAD ARE WITH US

RUDOLF STEINER

Sophia Books

Sophia Books
An imprint of Rudolf Steiner Press
Hillside House, The Square
Forest Row RH18 5ES

www.rudolfsteinerpress.com

Published by Rudolf Steiner Press 2006; reprinted 2014

First published by Rudolf Steiner Press in 1995 as part of the collection entitled *Life Beyond Death*

Originally published in German as part of the volume entitled *Der Tod als Lebenswandlung* (volume 182 in the *Rudolf Steiner Gesamtausgabe* or Collected Works) by Rudolf Steiner Verlag, Dornach. This authorized translation is published by permission of the Rudolf Steiner Nachlassverwaltung, Dornach

Translated by D.S. Osmond, and revised for this edition
This translation © Rudolf Steiner Press 1995

All rights reserved. No part of this publication may be reproduced, stored in a retrieval system, or transmitted, in any form or by any means, electronic, mechanical, photocopying or otherwise, without the prior permission of the publishers

A catalogue record for this book is available from the British Library

ISBN-10: 1 85584 104 5
ISBN-13: 978 1 85584 104 8

Cover by Andrew Morgan
Typeset by DP Photosetting, Aylesbury, Bucks.
Printed and bound in Great Britain by 4edge Limited, Essex

Contents

THE DEAD ARE WITH US
1

Notes
41

Further Reading
43

Publisher's Note on Rudolf Steiner's Lectures
45

In our study of spiritual science there is a great deal that we cannot, perhaps, directly apply in everyday life, and we may at times feel that it is all rather remote. But the remoteness is only apparent. The knowledge we gain about the secrets of the spiritual world is at every hour, at every moment, of vital and profound significance for our souls; what seems to be remote from us personally is often what the soul inwardly needs. In order to know the physical world we must make ourselves acquainted with it. But to know the spiritual world it is essential that we ourselves shall think through and master the thoughts and conceptions imparted by that world. These thoughts then often work quite unconsciously within the soul. Many things may seem to be remote, whereas in reality they are very near indeed to the higher realms of the soul's life.

And so again today we will think of the life that takes its course between death and a new birth—the life that seems so far removed from the human being in the physical world. I will begin by simply narrating what is found by spiritual investigation. These things can be understood if sufficient thought is applied to them; through their own power they make themselves comprehensible to the soul. Anyone who does not understand them should realize that he has not thought about them deeply enough. They must be *investigated* by means of spiritual science, but they can be *understood* through constant study. They will then be confirmed by the facts with which life itself confronts us, provided life is rightly observed.

You will have realized from many of the lecture-courses that study of the life between death and rebirth is fraught with difficulty, because its conditions are so entirely different from those of the life that can be pictured by the organs of the physical body here in the physical world. We have to become acquainted with utterly different conceptions.

When we enter into relationship with the things in our physical environment we know that only a small proportion of the beings around us in the physical world react to our deeds, to the manifestations of our will, in such a way that *pleasure* or *pain* is caused by these deeds of ours. Reaction of this kind takes place in the case of the animal kingdom and the human kingdom; but we are justified in the conviction that the mineral world (including what is contained in air and water), and also, largely, the world of plants, are insensitive to what we call pleasure or pain as the result of deeds performed by us. (Spiritually considered, of course, the matter is a little different, but that need not concern us at this point.) In the environment of the dead all this is changed. Conditions in the environment of the so-called dead are such that everything—

including what is done by the dead themselves—causes either pleasure or pain. The dead can do no single thing, they cannot—if I may speak pictorially—move a single limb without pleasure or pain being caused by what is done. We must try to think our way into these conditions of existence. We must assimilate the thought that life between death and a new birth is so constituted that everything we do awakens an echo in the environment. Through the whole period between death and a new birth we can do nothing, we cannot even move, metaphorically speaking, without causing pleasure or pain in our environment. The mineral kingdom as we have it around us on the physical plane does not exist for the dead, neither does the world of plants. As you can gather from my book *Theosophy*,[1] these kingdoms are present in an entirely different form. They are not present in the spiritual world in the form in which we know them here, as realms devoid of feeling.

The first kingdom of those familiar to us on

the physical plane that has significance for the dead, because it is comparable with what the deceased has in his environment, is the animal kingdom. I do not, of course, mean individual animals as we know them on the physical plane, but the whole environment is such that its effects and influences are as if animals were there. The reaction of the environment is such that pleasure or pain proceeds from what is done. On the physical plane we stand upon mineral soil; the dead stands upon a 'soil', lives in an environment, which may be compared with the animal nature in this sense. The deceased person therefore starts his life two kingdoms higher. On the earth we know the animal kingdom only from outside. The most external activity of the life between death and a new birth consists in acquiring a more and more intimate and exact knowledge [of the animal world].[2] For in this life between death and a new birth we must prepare all those forces which, working in from the cosmos, organize our own body. In the physical world we know nothing of these forces. Between death and a new birth we know that our body, down to its smallest particles, is formed out of the cosmos. For we ourselves prepare this physical body, bringing together in it the whole of animal nature; we ourselves build it.

To make the picture more exact, we must acquaint ourselves with an idea that is rather remote from contemporary views. Modern man knows quite well that when a magnetic needle lies with one end pointing towards the north and the other towards the south, this is not caused by the needle itself; the earth as a whole is a cosmic magnet of which one end points towards the north and the other towards the south. It would be considered sheer nonsense to say that the direction is determined by forces contained in the magnetic needle itself. In the case of a seed or germinating entity which develops in an animal or in a human being, all the sciences and schools of thought deny the factor of cosmic influence. What would be described as nonsense in the case of the magnetic needle is accepted without further thought in the case of an egg forming inside the hen. But when the egg is forming inside the hen, the whole cosmos is, in fact, participating; what happens on earth merely provides the stimulus for the operation of cosmic forces. Everything that takes shape in the egg is an imprint of cosmic forces and the hen herself is only a place, an abode, in which the cosmos, the whole universe, is working in this way. And it is the same in the case of the human being. This is a thought with which we must become familiar.

Between death and a new birth, in communion with beings of the higher hierarchies, a person is working at this whole system of forces permeating the cosmos. For between death and a new birth he is not inactive; he is perpetually at work—in the spiritual. The animal kingdom is the first realm with which he makes acquaintance, and in the following way. If he commits some error he immediately becomes aware of pain, of suffering, in the environment; if he does something right, he becomes aware of pleasure, of joy, in the environment. He works on and on, calling forth pleasure or pain, until finally the soul is such that it can descend and unite with what will live on earth as a physical body. The being of soul could never descend if it had not itself worked at the physical form.

It is the animal kingdom, then, with which acquaintance is made in the first place. The next is the human kingdom. Mineral nature and the plant kingdom are absent. Acquaintance with the human kingdom is limited: between death and a new birth—and this begins immediately or soon after death—the soul has contact and can make links only with those human souls, whether still living on earth or in yonder world, with whom he has already been karmically connected on earth in the last or in an earlier incarnation. Other souls pass him by; they do not come within his ken. He becomes aware of the animal realm as a totality; only those human souls come within his ken with whom he has had some karmic connection here on earth, and with these he becomes more and more closely acquainted. You must not imagine that their number is small, for individual human beings have already passed through many lives on the earth. In every life numbers of karmic connections have been formed and of these is spun the web which then, in the spiritual world, connects all the souls whom the dead has known in life; only those with whom no acquaintance has been made remain outside the circle.

This indicates a truth which must be emphasized, namely the supreme importance of earthly life for the individual human being. If there had been no earthly life we should be unable to form links with human souls in the spiritual world. The links are formed karmically on the earth and then continue between death and a new birth. Those who are able to see into the spiritual world perceive how the dead person gradually makes more and more links—all of which are the outcome of karmic connections formed on earth.

Just as we can say of the first kingdom with which the dead come into contact—the animal kingdom—that everything the dead do, even when they simply move, causes either pleasure or pain in their environment, so we can say about everything experienced in the human realm in yonder world that it is much more intimately connected with the life of soul. When the deceased becomes acquainted with a soul, he gets to know this soul as if he himself were within it. After death, knowledge of another soul is as intimate as knowledge here on earth of our own finger, head or ear—we feel ourselves within the other soul. The connection is much more intimate than it can ever be on earth.

There are two basic experiences in the community among human souls between death and a new birth; we are either within the other souls or outside them. Even in the case of souls with whom we are already acquainted, we are sometimes within and sometimes outside them. Meeting with them consists in feeling at one with them, being within them; to be outside them means that we do not notice them, do not become aware of them. If we look at some object here on earth, we perceive it; if we look away from it, we no longer perceive it. In yonder world we are actually within human souls when we are able to turn our attention to them; and we are outside them when we are not in a position to do so.

What I have now said is an indication of the fundamental form of the soul's communion with other souls during the period between death and a new birth. Similarly, the human being is also within or outside the beings of the hierarchies, the Angeloi, Archangeloi, and so on. The higher the kingdoms, the more intensely does the human being feel bound to them after death; he feels as though they were bearing him, sustaining him, with great power. The Archangeloi are a mightier support than the Angeloi, the Archai again mightier than the Archangeloi, and so on.

People today still find difficulties in acquiring knowledge of the spiritual world. The difficulties would soon resolve themselves if a little more trouble were taken to become acquainted with its secrets. There are two ways of approach. One way leads to complete certainty of the eternal in one's own being. This knowledge, that in human nature there is an eternal core of being which passes through birth and death—this knowledge, remote as it is to the modern mind, is comparatively easy to attain; and it will certainly be attained by those who have enough perseverance, along the path described in the book *Knowledge of the Higher Worlds*,[3] and in other writings. It is attained by treading the path there described. That is one form of knowledge of the spiritual world. The other is what may be called direct communication with beings of the spiritual world, and we will now speak of the communication that is possible between those still living on earth and the so-called dead.

Such communication is most certainly possible but it presents greater difficulties than the first form of knowledge, which is easy to attain.

Actual communication with an individual who has died is possible, but difficult, because it demands scrupulous vigilance on the part of the one who seeks to establish it. Control and discipline are necessary for this kind of intercourse with the spiritual world, because it is connected with a very significant law. Impulses recognized as lower impulses in people on earth are, from the spiritual side, higher life; and it may therefore easily happen that when the human being has not achieved true control of himself, he experiences the rising of lower impulses as the result of direct communication with the dead. When we make contact with the spiritual world in a general sense, when we acquire knowledge about our own immortality as beings of soul and spirit, there can be no question of the ingress of anything impure. But when it is a matter of contact with individuals who have died, the relationship with the deceased individual—strange as it seems—is always a relationship with the blood and nervous system. The dead enter into those impulses which live themselves out in the system of blood and nerves, and in this way lower impulses may be aroused. Naturally, there is only danger for those who have not purified their natures through discipline and control. This must be said, for it is the reason why in the Old Testament it is forbidden to have communication with the dead.[4] Such intercourse is not sinful when it happens in the right way. The methods of modern spiritualism must, of course, be avoided. When the intercourse is of a spiritual nature it is not sinful, but when it is not accompanied by pure thoughts it can easily lead to the stimulation of lower passions. It is not the dead who arouse these passions but the element in which the dead live. For consider this: what we feel here as 'animal' in quality and nature is the basic element in which the dead live. The kingdom in which the dead live can easily be changed when it enters into us; what is higher life in yonder world can become lower impulses when it is within us on earth. It is very important to remember this, and it must be emphasized when we are speaking of communication between the living and the so-called dead, for it is an occult fact. We shall find that precisely when we are speaking about this communication, the spiritual world can be described as it really is, for such experiences reveal that the spiritual world is completely different from the physical world.

To begin with, I will tell you something that may seem to have no meaning until we have developed faculties of clairvoyance; but when we think it over we shall realize that it concerns us closely. Those who are able to commune with the dead as the result of developed clairvoyance realize why it is so difficult for human beings to know anything about the dead through direct perception. Strange as it may seem, the whole form of communication to which we are accustomed in the physical world has to be reversed when intercourse is established between the earth and the dead. In the physical world, when we speak to a human being from physical body to physical body, we know that the words come from ourselves; when the other person speaks to us, we know that the words come from him. The whole relationship is reversed when we are speaking with one who has died. The expression 'when we are speaking' can truthfully be used, but the relationship is reversed. When we put a question to the dead, or say something to him, what we say comes from *him*, comes to us from him. He inspires in our soul what we ask him, what we say to him. And when he answers us or says something to us, this comes out of our own soul. It is a process with which a human being in the physical world is quite unfamiliar. He feels that what he says comes out of his own being. In order to establish communication with those who have died, we must adapt ourselves to hear from them what we ourselves say, and to receive from our own soul what they answer.

Thus abstractly described, the nature of the process is easy to grasp; but to become accustomed to the total reversal of the familiar form of intercourse is exceedingly difficult. The dead are always there, always among us and around us, and the fact that they are not perceived is largely due to lack of understanding of this reversed form of communication. On the physical plane we think that when anything comes out of our soul, it comes from us. And we are far from being able to pay intimate enough attention to whether it is not, after all, being inspired in us from the spiritual environment. We prefer to connect it with experiences familiar on the physical plane, where, if something comes to us from the environment, we ascribe it at once to the other person. This is the greatest error when it is a matter of intercourse with the dead.

This is one of the fundamental principles of communication between the so-called living and the so-called dead. If this example helps you to realize one thing only, namely, that conditions are entirely reversed in the spiritual world, then you will have grasped a very significant concept and one that is constantly needed by those who aspire to become conscious of the spiritual world. The concept is extremely difficult to apply in an actual, individual case. For instance, in order to understand even the physical world, permeated as it is with the spiritual, it is essential to grasp this idea of complete reversal. And because modern science fails to grasp it and it is altogether unfamiliar to ordinary consciousness, there is today no spiritual understanding of the physical world. One experiences this even with people who try very hard indeed to comprehend the world and one is often obliged simply to accept the situation and leave it as it is. Some years ago I was speaking to a large number of friends at a meeting in Berlin about the human physical organism, with special reference to certain ideas of Goethe. I tried to explain how the head, in respect of its physical structure, can only be rightly understood when it is conceived as a complete transformation of the other part of the organism.[5] No one was able to understand at all that a bone in the arm would have to be turned inside out like a glove, in order to give rise to a skull-bone. It is a difficult concept, but one cannot really understand anatomy without such pictures. I mention this in parenthesis only. What I have said today about communication with the dead is easier to understand.

The phenomena I have described to you are going on all the time. All of you sitting here now are in constant communication with the dead, only ordinary consciousness knows nothing of it because it lies in the subconscious. Clairvoyant consciousness does not initiate anything new but merely brings to consciousness what is present all the time in the spiritual world. All of you are in constant communication with the dead.

And now we will consider how this communication takes place in individual cases. When someone has died and we are left behind, we may ask: how do I approach the one who has died, so that he is aware of me? How does he come near me again so that I can live in him? These questions may well be asked but they cannot be answered if we have recourse only to concepts familiar on the physical plane. On the physical plane, ordinary consciousness functions only from the time of waking until the time of falling asleep; but the other part of consciousness which remains dim in ordinary life between falling asleep and waking is just as important. The human being is not, properly speaking, unconscious when he is asleep; his consciousness is merely so dim that he experiences nothing. But the whole human being—in waking and sleeping life—must be held in mind when we are studying the connections of the human being with the spiritual world. Think of your own biography. Your reflections on the course of your life always contain interruptions; you describe only what has happened in your waking hours. Life is broken: waking-sleeping; waking-sleeping. But you are also present while you sleep; and in studying the whole human being, both waking life and sleeping life must be taken into consideration.

A third thing must also be held in mind in connection with our communications with the spiritual world. For besides waking life and sleeping life there is a third state, even more important for intercourse with the spiritual world than waking and sleeping life as such. I mean the state connected with the act of waking and the act of going to sleep, which lasts only for brief seconds, for we immediately pass on into other conditions. If we develop a delicate sensitivity for these moments of waking and going to sleep we shall find that they shed great light on the spiritual world. In remote country places—although such customs are gradually disappearing—when we who are older were still young, people were wont to say: when you wake from sleep it is not good immediately to go to the window through which light is streaming; you should stay a little while in the dark. Country folk used to have some knowledge about contact with the spiritual world and at this moment of waking they preferred not to come at once into bright daylight but to remain inwardly collected, in order to preserve something of what sweeps with such power through the human soul at the moment of waking. The sudden brightness of daylight is disturbing. In the cities, of course, this is hardly to be avoided; there we are disturbed not only by the daylight but also even before waking by the noise from the streets, the clanging of tramcar bells and so forth. The whole of civilized life seems to conspire to hinder our contact with the spiritual world. This is not said in order to decry material civilization, but the facts must be remembered. Again, at the moment of going to sleep, the spiritual world approaches us with power, but we immediately fall asleep, losing consciousness of what has passed through the soul. Exceptions do, of course, occur. These moments of waking and of going to sleep are of the utmost significance for communication with the so-called dead—and with other spiritual beings of the higher worlds. But in order to understand what I have to say about this you must familiarize yourselves with an idea which is not easy to apply on the physical plane and which is therefore practically unknown. It is as follows.

In the spiritual sense, what is 'past' has not really vanished but is still there. In physical life people have this conception in regard to space only. If you stand in front of a tree, then go away and look back at it later on, the tree has not disappeared; it is still there. In the spiritual world the same is true in regard to time. If you experience something at one moment, it has passed away the next as far as physical consciousness is concerned; spiritually conceived, it has not passed away. You can look back at it just as you looked back at the tree. Richard Wagner showed that he had knowledge of this in the remarkable words: 'Time here becomes space.'[6] It is an occult fact that in the spiritual world there are degrees of distance which do not come to expression on the physical plane. That an event is past simply means that it is farther away from us. I beg you to remember this. For man on earth in the physical body, the moment of going to sleep is 'past' when the moment of waking arrives. In the spiritual world, however, the moment of falling asleep has not gone; we are only, at the moment of waking, a little further distant from it. We encounter our dead at the moment of going to sleep and again at the moment of waking. (As I said, this is perpetually happening, only it usually remains in the subconscious.) As far as physical consciousness is concerned, these are two quite different moments in time; for spiritual consciousness the one is only a little farther distant than the other. I want you to remember this in connection with what I am now going to say, otherwise you may find it difficult to understand.

As I told you, the moments of waking and going to sleep are particularly important for contact with those who have died. Through the whole of our life there are no such moments when we do not come into relation with the dead.

The moment of going to sleep is especially favourable for us to turn to the dead. Suppose we want to ask the dead something. We can carry it in our soul, holding it until the moment of going to sleep, for that is the time to bring our questions to the dead. Other opportunities exist, but this moment is the most favourable. When, for instance, we read to the dead we certainly draw near to them, but for direct communication it is best of all if we put our questions to them at the moment of going to sleep.

On the other hand, the moment of waking is the most favourable for what the dead have to communicate to us. And again there is no one— did people but know it—who at the moment of waking does not bring with him countless tidings from the dead. In the subconscious region of the soul we are speaking continually with the dead. At the moment of going to sleep we put our questions to them, we say to them what, in the depths of the soul, we have to say. At the moment of waking the dead speak with us, give us the answers. But we must realize that these are only two different points and that, in the higher sense, these things that happen after each other are really simultaneous, just as on the physical plane two places are there simultaneously.

Some factors in life are favourable for contact with the dead, others are less so. And we may ask: what can really help us to establish communication with the dead? The manner of our converse cannot be the same as it is with those who are alive, for the dead neither hears nor takes in this kind of speech. There is no question of being able to chatter with one who has died as we chatter with one another at tea or in cafés. What makes it possible to put questions to the dead or to communicate something to him is that we unite the life of *feeling* with our thoughts and ideas. Suppose a person has passed through the gate of death and you want your subconscious to communicate something to him in the evening. It need not be communicated consciously; you can prepare it at some time during the day. Then, if you go to bed at ten o'clock at night having prepared it, say, at noon, it passes over to the dead when you go to sleep. The question must, however, be put in a particular way; it must not merely be a thought or an idea, it must be imbued with feeling and with will. Your relationship with the dead must be one of the heart, of inner interest. You must remind yourself of your love for the person when he was alive and address yourself to him with real warmth of heart, not abstractly. This feeling can take such firm root in the soul that in the evening, at the moment of going to sleep, it becomes a question to the dead without your knowing it. Or you may try to realize vividly what was the nature of your particular interest in the one who has died. Think about your experiences with him; visualize actual moments when you were together with him, and then ask yourself: what was it about him that particularly interested me, that attracted me to him? When was it that I was so deeply impressed, liked what he said, found it helpful and valuable?

If you remind yourself of moments when you were strongly connected with the dead person and were deeply interested in him, and then turn this into a desire to speak to him, to say something to him—if you develop the feeling with purity of heart and let the question arise out of the interest you took in him, then the question remains in your soul, and when you go to sleep it passes over to him. Ordinary consciousness as a rule will know little of this, because sleep ensues immediately. But what has thus passed over often remains present in dreams.

In the case of most dreams—although in respect of actual content they are misleading—in the case of most dreams we have of the dead, all that happens is that we interpret them incorrectly. We interpret them as messages from the dead, whereas they are nothing but the echoing of the questions or communications we have ourselves directed to the dead. We should not think that the person who has died is saying something to us in our dream, but we should see in the dream something that goes out from our own soul to the dead person. The dream is the echo of this. If we were sufficiently developed to be conscious of our question or communication to the dead at the moment of going to sleep, it would seem to us as though the dead person himself were speaking—hence the echo in the dream seems as if it were a message from him. In reality it comes from ourselves. This becomes intelligible only when we understand the nature of clairvoyant connection with the dead. What the dead seem to say to us is really what we are saying to them.

The moment of waking is especially favourable for the dead to approach us. At the moment of waking, very much comes from the dead to every human being. A great deal of what we undertake in life is really inspired in us by the dead or by beings of the higher hierarchies, although we attribute it to ourselves, imagining that it comes from our own soul. The life of day draws near, the moment of waking passes quickly by, and we seldom pay heed to the intimate indications that arise out of our soul. And when we do, we are vain enough to attribute them to ourselves. Yet in all this—and in much else that comes out of our own soul—there lives what the dead have to say to us. It is indeed so: what the dead say to us seems as if it arises out of our own soul. If people knew what life truly is, this knowledge would engender a feeling of reverence and piety towards the spiritual world in which we are always living, together with the dead with whom we are connected. We should realize that in much of what we do, the dead are working. The knowledge that around us, like the very air we breathe, there is a spiritual world, the knowledge that the dead are round about us only we are not able to perceive them—this knowledge must arise in spiritual science not as theory but so that it permeates the soul as inner life. The dead speak to us inwardly but we interpret our own inner life incorrectly. If we were to understand it aright, we should know that in our inmost being we are united with the souls who are the so-called dead.

Now it is not at all the same when a soul passes through the gate of death in relatively early years or later in life. The death of young children who have loved us is a very different thing from the death of people older than ourselves. Experience of the spiritual world shows that the secret of communion with children who have died can be expressed by saying that in the spiritual sense we do not lose them, they remain with us. When children die in early life they continue to be with us—spiritually with us. I should like to give this to you as a theme for meditation, that when little children die they are not lost to us; we do not lose them, they stay with us spiritually. Of older people who die, the opposite may be said. Those who are older do not lose us. *We* do not lose little children; elderly people do not lose *us*. When elderly people die they are strongly drawn to the spiritual world, but this also gives them the power so to work into the physical world that it is easier for them to approach us. True, they withdraw much farther from the physical world than do children who remain near us, but they are endowed with higher faculties of perception than children who die young. Knowledge of different souls in the spiritual world reveals that those who died in old age are able to enter easily into souls on earth; they do not lose the souls on earth. And we do not lose little children, for they remain more or less within the sphere of earthly man. The meaning of the difference can also be considered in another respect.

We do not always have sufficient insight into the experiences of the soul on the physical plane. When friends die, we mourn and feel pain. When good friends pass away, I have often said that it is not the task of anthroposophy to offer people shallow consolation for their pain or try to talk them out of their sorrow. One should grow strong enough to bear sorrow; not allow oneself to be talked out of it. But people make no distinction as to whether the sorrow is caused by the death of a child or of one who is elderly. Spiritually perceived, there is a very great difference. When little children have died, the pain of those who have remained behind is really a kind of compassion—no matter whether such children were their own or other children whom they loved. Children remain with us and because we have been united with them they convey their pain to our souls; we feel their pain—that they would prefer to still be here! Their pain is eased when we bear it with them. The child feels in us, shares his feeling with us, and it is good that it should be so; his pain is thereby softened.

On the other hand, the pain we feel at the death of elderly people—whether relatives or friends—can be called egotistical pain. An elderly person who has died does not lose us and the feeling he has is therefore different from the feeling present in a child. One who dies in later life does not lose us. We here in life feel that we have lost him—the pain is therefore *ours*; it is egotistical pain. We do not share his feeling as we do in the case of children; we feel the pain for ourselves.

A clear distinction can therefore be made between these two forms of pain: egotistical pain in connection with the elderly; pain fraught with compassion in connection with little children. The child lives on in us and we actually feel what he feels. In reality, our own soul mourns only for those who died in the later years of their life.

It is a matter such as this that can show us the immense significance of knowledge of the spiritual world. For you see, a religious service for the dead can be adapted in accordance with these truths. In the case of a child who has died, it will not be altogether appropriate to emphasize the individual aspect. Because the child lives on in us and remains with us, the service of remembrance should take a more universal form, giving the child, who is still near us, something that is wide and universal. Therefore in the case of a child, a simple ceremony in the service is preferable to a special funeral oration. The Catholic ritual is better here in one respect, the Protestant in the other. The Catholic service includes no funeral oration but consists of ceremony, ritual. It is general, universal, alike for all. And what can be alike for all is especially good for children. But in the case of one who has died in later years, the individual aspect is more important. The best funeral service here will be one in which the life of the individual is remembered. The Protestant service, with the oration referring to the life of the one who has died, will have great significance for the soul; the Catholic ritual will mean less in such a case.

The same distinction holds good for all our thoughts about those who have died. It is best for a child when we engender a mood of feeling connected with him; we try to turn our thoughts to him and these thoughts will draw near to him when we sleep. Such thoughts may be of a more general kind—such for example as may be directed to all those who have passed through the gate of death. In the case of an elderly person, we must direct our thoughts of remembrance to him as an individual, thinking about his life on earth and of experiences we shared with him. In order to establish the right contact with an older person it is very important to visualize him as he actually was, to make his being come to life in ourselves—not only by remembering things he said which meant a great deal to us but by thinking of what he was as an individual and what his value was for the world. If we make these things inwardly alive, they will enable us to come into connection with an older person who has died and to have the right thoughts of remembrance for him. So you see, it is important to know what attitude should be taken to those who have died in childhood and to those who have died in the later years of life.

Just think what it means at the present time, when so many human beings are dying at a comparatively young age,[7] to be able to say to oneself: they are really always present, they are not lost to the world. (I have spoken of this from other points of view, for such matters must always be considered from different angles.) If we succeed in becoming conscious of the spiritual world, one realization at least will light up in us out of the deep sorrow with which the present time is fraught. It is that because those who die young remain with us, a living spiritual life can arise through community with the dead. A living spiritual life can and will arise, if only materialism is not allowed to become so strong that Ahriman is able to stretch out his claws and gain the victory over all human powers.

Many people may say, speaking purely of conditions on the physical plane, that indications such as I have been giving seem very remote; they would prefer to be told definitely what they can do in the morning and evening in order to bring themselves into a right relation with the spiritual world. But this is not quite correct. Where the spiritual world is concerned, the first essential is that we should develop thoughts about it. And even if it seems as though the dead are far away, while immediate life is close at hand, the very fact that we have such thoughts as have been described today and that we allow our minds to dwell on things seemingly remote from external life—this very fact uplifts the soul, imparts to it spiritual strength and spiritual nourishment. Do not, therefore, be afraid of thinking these thoughts through again and again, continually bringing them to new life within the soul. *There is nothing more important for life, even for material life, than the strong and sure realization of communion with the spiritual world.*

If modern people had not lost their relationship with spiritual things to such an extent, these grave times would not have come upon us. Only a very few today have insight into this connection, although it will certainly be recognized in the future. Today people think: when a human being has passed through the gate of death, his activity ceases as far as the physical world is concerned. But indeed it is not so! There is a living and perpetual intercourse between the so-called dead and the so-called living. These who have passed through the gate of death have not ceased to be present; it is only that our eyes have ceased to see them. They are there in very truth.

Our thoughts, our feelings, our impulses of will, are all connected with the dead. The words of the Gospel hold good for the dead as well: 'The kingdom of the Spirit cometh not with observation' (that is to say, external observation); 'neither shall they say, Lo here, lo there, for, behold, the kingdom of the Spirit is within you.'[8] We should not seek for the dead through externalities but become conscious that they are always present. All history, all social dynamics, all ethical life, proceed by virtue of cooperation between the so-called living and the so-called dead. The whole human being can be infinitely strengthened when he is conscious not only of his firm stand here in the physical world but is filled with the inner realization of being able to say of the dead whom he has loved: they are with us, they are in our midst.

This, too, is part of a true knowledge and understanding of the spiritual world which has, as it were, to be woven from many different threads. We cannot say that we *know* the spiritual world until the way in which we think and speak about it comes from that world itself.

The dead are in our midst—these words in themselves are an affirmation of the spiritual world; and only the spiritual world itself can awaken within us the consciousness that in very truth the dead are with us.

Notes

The text is a record of a lecture Rudolf Steiner gave to members of the Anthroposophical Society in Nuremberg on 10 February 1918.

GA = *Gesamtausgabe*: the Collected Works of Rudolf Steiner in the original German.

1. GA 9. *Theosophy*, Rudolf Steiner Press 1973.
2. The square brackets have been added by the editor.
3. GA 10. *Knowledge of the Higher Worlds*, Rudolf Steiner Press 1969.
4. In the fifth Book of Moses, chapter 18, verse 10: 'There shall not be found among you any one ... that useth divination or ... a consulter with familiar spirits ... For all that do these things are an abomination unto the Lord ...' See also the first Book of Samuel, chapter 28 (Samuel and the witch of Endor).

5. See *The Wisdom of Man, of the Soul and of the Spirit*, 12 lectures, Berlin 1909–11 (GA 115), Anthroposophic Press 1971.
6. Richard Wagner, 1813–83. See *Parsifal*, Scene 1:
   Parsifal: I hardly take one pace
                 and yet it seems I journey far.
   Gurnemanz: It is so my son, for you see
                 that time here becomes space.
7. This lecture was given by Steiner during the First World War. It is worth noting that most academic sources agree that military deaths alone during that conflict totalled 8,500,000!
8. Luke 17: 20–21.

Further Reading

Rudolf Steiner's fundamental books:

Knowledge of the Higher Words
also published as: *How to Know Higher Worlds*

Occult Science
also published as: *An Outline of Esoteric Science*

Theosophy

The Philosophy of Freedom
also published as:
Intuitive Thinking as a Spiritual Path

Some relevant volumes of Rudolf Steiner's verses and lectures:

Life Beyond Death
Staying Connected
Living With the Dead
Manifestations of Karma

For all titles contact Rudolf Steiner Press (UK) or SteinerBooks (USA):
www.rudolfsteinerpress.com www.steinerbooks.org

Publisher's Note on Rudolf Steiner's Lectures

The lectures and addresses contained in this volume have been translated from the German, which is based on stenographic and other recorded texts that were in most cases never seen or revised by the lecturer. Hence, due to human errors in hearing and transcription, they may contain mistakes and faulty passages. Every effort has been made to ensure that this is not the case. Some of the lectures were given to audiences more familiar with anthroposophy; these are the so-called 'private' or 'members' lectures. Other lectures, like the written works, were intended for the general public. The difference between these, as Rudolf Steiner indicates in his *Autobiography*, is twofold. On the one hand, the members' lectures take for granted a background in and commitment to anthroposophy; in the public lectures this was not the case. At the same time, the members' lectures address the concerns and dilemmas of the members, while the public work speaks directly out of

Steiner's own understanding of universal needs. Nevertheless, as Rudolf Steiner stresses: 'Nothing was ever said that was not solely the result of my direct experience of the growing content of anthroposophy. There was never any question of concessions to the prejudices and preferences of the members. Whoever reads these privately printed lectures can take them to represent anthroposophy in the fullest sense. Thus it was possible without hesitation—when the complaints in this direction became too persistent—to depart from the custom of circulating this material "For members only". But it must be borne in mind that faulty passages do occur in these reports not revised by myself.' Earlier in the same chapter, he states: 'Had I been able to correct them [*the private lectures*], the restriction *for members only* would have been unnecessary from the beginning.'

The original German editions on which this text is based were published by Rudolf Steiner Verlag, Dornach, Switzerland in the collected edition (*Gesamtausgabe*, 'GA') of Rudolf Steiner's work. All publications are edited by the Rudolf Steiner Nachlassverwaltung (estate), which wholly owns both Rudolf Steiner Verlag and the Rudolf Steiner Archive. The organization relies solely on donations to continue its activity.

Other budget-priced volumes from Rudolf Steiner Press

Single lectures:
How Can I Find the Christ?
The Work of the Angel in Our Astral Body

Meditations:
Calendar of the Soul, The Year Participated
The Foundation Stone Meditation